2013 BOSTON MARATHON

SPORTS UNITE US

2013 BOSTON MARATHON

Published in the United States of America by Cherry Lake Publishing
Ann Arbor, Michigan
www.cherrylakepublishing.com

Reading Adviser: Marla Conn MS, Ed., Literacy specialist, Read-Ability, Inc.

Photo Credits: ©Marcio Jose Bastos Silva/Shutterstock, cover; ©Jim Rogash/Getty Images, 1; ©Marcio Jose Bastos Silva/Shutterstock, 5; ©Songquan Deng/Shutterstock, 6; ©Jaminnbenji/Shutterstock, 8; ©Tom Green/ZUMAPRESS/Newscom, 11; ©Kevork Djansezian/Getty Images, 12; ©2nd Lt. Matthew Feehan/ DoD/Sipa USA/Newscom, 15; ©Alex Trautwig/Getty Images, 16; ©Paul Marotta/Getty Images, 17; ©Nicolaus Czarnecki/ZUMA Wire/Newscom, 21; ©Dave Sandford/Pool/Getty Images, 22; ©Christopher Penler/Shutterstock, 25; ©Jim Rogash/Getty Images, 28; ©Jim Rogash/Getty Images, 28; ©Spencer Platt/ Getty Images, 29; ©Darren McCollester/Getty Images, 29; ©Jaminnbenji/Shutterstock, 30

Library of Congress Cataloging-in-Publication Data has been filed and is available at catalog.loc.gov

Cherry Lake Publishing would like to acknowledge the work of The Partnership for 21st Century Learning.
Please visit *www.p21.org* for more information.

Printed in the United States of America
Corporate Graphics

ABOUT THE AUTHOR

Heather Williams is a writer and educator with a passion for seeing readers of all ages connect with others through stories and personal experiences. She enjoys running, reading, and watching sports. Heather lives in Greensboro, North Carolina with her husband and two children.

TABLE OF CONTENTS

CHAPTER 1

The Starting Block

A marathon is a 26.2-mile (42.2-kilometer) foot race. The first marathon was held at the very first **modern** Olympic Games in 1896 in Athens, Greece. More than 1 million people around the globe participate in marathons each year. Run clubs meet each week to train together. Volunteers pass out water to runners at races. **Spectators** gather on the sidelines to cheer for runners. Some marathons raise money for charities. Other marathons help runners qualify for the Olympics. One of those races is the Boston Marathon. The Boston Marathon is the oldest **annual** marathon in the world. In 2013, a **tragedy** took place at the Boston Marathon.

The Boston Marathon draws elite runners from all over the world.

Boston is the capital city of Massachusetts. It is also the home of one of the world's most famous marathons. The first Boston Marathon took place in 1897. There were only 15 runners in the first race. It is held every April on Patriots' Day, the third Monday in April. Runners from all over the world compete in the Boston Marathon. The race route goes through many Boston neighborhoods. It takes runners past several Boston landmarks, such as Boston College.

Fenway Park, home of the Boston Red Sox, is next to the final stretch of the Boston Marathon.

There are many traditions that make the Boston Marathon special. Every year on marathon day, the Boston Red Sox have a morning baseball game. Baseball fans can watch the game and see the runners entering the final stretch of the marathon. Around the halfway mark of the race is the Wellesley "Scream Tunnel." Wellesley College is an all-women's college in Boston. Students from the college line the route and scream at the runners going by. They also hold signs asking for kisses and high fives. The Boston Marathon's male and female winners receive **olive wreaths** from Marathon, Greece. This gesture honors the

ancient Olympics and the site of the first marathon.

More than 20,000 runners compete in the Boston Marathon each year. Hundreds of volunteers help with the race. Medical tents and emergency crews are stationed along the route. Around 1 million people come to watch the marathon. Spectators are allowed to line up behind fencing along every mile of the race. Friends and family can sign up for phone alerts to track specific runners. Because so many people gather for the marathon, security measures are very important.

Qualifying

*Runners hoping to race in the Olympics must **qualify** in a race **sanctioned** by USA Track & Field. The Boston Marathon is a sanctioned race. A runner's Boston Marathon finishing time can qualify them for the United States Olympic track and field team. A male runner must finish the marathon in 2 hours and 19 minutes. A female runner must finish in 2 hours and 45 minutes. An athlete who has qualified at Boston or another sanctioned course can then run in the Olympic **trials**.*

With thousands of runners and over a million spectators, security is an important part of the Boston Marathon.

Boston participates in a program called Urban Shield. It is a training program that helps police, emergency responders, and citizens prepare for a citywide emergency. Urban Shield involves a fake emergency that puts the entire city through a test. Before the city could experience the test emergency, Boston faced a real emergency at the finish line of the 2013 Boston Marathon.

Women in the Boston Marathon

The **Amateur** Athletic Union (AAU) did not allow women to register for marathons until 1971. AAU officials believed women were too **fragile** to run long distances. Women were only allowed to run 800 meters or less in the Olympics and other races. But in 1966, a runner named Roberta Gibb became the first woman to run in the Boston Marathon. She hid in the bushes and joined the other runners after the race started. The next year, a woman named Kathrine Switzer registered for the Boston Marathon. She did not put her gender on the race application. When race officials realized she was a woman, they tried to remove her from the race. The Boston Marathon officially allowed women to register in 1972. Switzer and seven other women finished the race that year. Switzer has run 39 marathons. She finished second in the Boston Marathon in 1975.

CHAPTER 2

The Finish Line

By 11:00 a.m. on April 15, 2013, all of the race's 26,000 participants had started the race. At around 2:50 p.m., two homemade bombs exploded at the finish line. The explosions were 12 seconds apart. They were between 50 and 100 yards (46 and 91 meters) away from each other. The bombs were inside large backpacks left on the ground among spectators. Three spectators were killed by the bombs. More than 260 people were injured.

The bombs were made by two brothers, Tamerlan and Dzhokhar Tsarnaev. Dzhokhar was a student at the University of Massachusetts Dartmouth. Tamerlan was seven years older. He wanted to become a professional boxer. The brothers got help

Smoke fills the air as the first bomb explodes in the crowd near the finish line.

from their roommates. Dzhokhar said the brothers made the bombs because they believed Muslims around the world were mistreated.

After the explosions, the brothers went back to their normal lives. Three days later, the Federal Bureau of Investigation (FBI) published photos of the bombing suspects. The Tsarnaev brothers gathered guns and explosives. They ran from police in Tamerlan's car. At the Massachusetts Institute of Technology (MIT), Tamerlan killed a police officer. The brothers tried to take the

It took nine days to reopen Boyleston Street after the bombing.

officer's gun and left Tamerlan's car behind. They stole a car and shot at the police during a chase. Tamerlan was killed in the chase.

Dzhokhar escaped, even though he had also been shot by police. Residents of Boston were told to stay inside their houses. Officers walked door to door in a city called Watertown looking for him. A man heard a noise in his backyard and went outside to see what it was. He saw a man covered in blood hiding under a tarp in his yard. When the police came, they identified the man under the tarp as Dzhokhar.

Dzhokhar was given a trial by jury in 2015. He admitted his crime and was sentenced to death. Several of the brothers' friends and roommates were also investigated. Many of them were sentenced to prison and fined. Some of them were charged with helping the brothers commit a violent crime. Others were accused of hiding evidence and lying to police.

Patriots' Day

There are two holidays in the U.S. with similar names. They are Patriot Day and Patriots' Day. Patriot Day is September 11 and honors the victims of the 2001 terrorist attack. Patriots' Day is observed the third Monday of April. It is only a holiday in Massachusetts and Maine. Patriots' Day honors the Battles of Lexington and Concord. These battles were fought outside Boston in 1775. The Battles of Lexington and Concord were the start of the American Revolutionary War (1775–1783). The Boston Marathon takes place on Patriots' Day each year.

The Kindness of Strangers

People came together to help in many ways moments after the bombs went off. Runners who were nearing the end of the race **sprinted** to the aid of others. Many runners went straight to the medical tent to give blood. Spectators who were not hurt helped get injured people to safety. Some residents even ran from their homes and into the street to offer a hand. Many police and emergency medical workers were at the scene. However, they relied on help from ordinary people to assist those who were hurt.

Fifteen members of the Massachusetts National Guard had already finished the marathon. They had run the race carrying 40-pound (18-kilogram) military backpacks filled with

Members of the Massachusetts National Guard receive instructions on the afternoon of the bombing.

supplies. They were running to honor soldiers who were killed in Iraq and Afghanistan. When they heard the bomb, they took action. The guardsmen pulled down a fence so medical workers could get to victims. They helped remove debris from around injured people.

One of the soldiers being honored by the Massachusetts National Guard was Alex Arredondo. Alex was killed in Iraq during a war. His father, Carlos, was a volunteer at the 2013 Boston Marathon. Arredondo heard the blasts and looked around

Strangers comfort each other at the finish line.

to see who needed help. He saw a young man lying on the ground. There were flames around him, and he was bleeding. Arredondo put out the flames and tried to stop the bleeding in the man's leg. He called for a wheelchair and someone brought one from the medical tent. Arredondo put the young man in the wheelchair and rushed him to an ambulance.

Dr. Chris Rupe had come to Boston to run the marathon. He finished the race a few seconds before the first blast. Rupe turned and ran back toward the finish line. He wanted to help. Rupe was sent to the race's medical tent. There, he helped other

Joe Andruzzi, former New England Patriots lineman, called firefighters, medics, EMTs, and police officers the real heroes of April 15, 2013.

doctors and volunteers with the injured. He treated minor cuts and burns. Rupe helped prepare patients with severe injuries for the ambulance ride to a local hospital.

Dr. Vivek Shah was a few yards from finishing the Boston Marathon when he heard an explosion. At first, he thought it was fireworks. Then he saw spectators running away. He ran to the site of the explosions to help. Shah was one of many volunteer doctors who were trying to help at the finish line. He helped other doctors treat injuries.

A team of runners in the 2013 Boston Marathon were running for the Joe Andruzzi Foundation. This organization helps pay for treatment for children with brain cancer. It was started by former New England Patriots lineman Joe Andruzzi. Andruzzi was near the finish line when the bombs exploded. He helped carry many victims to safety.

Andruzzi said he was not a hero that day. Instead, Andruzzi praised the hundreds of volunteers, runners, and first responders who acted on behalf of others. Many people united to help strangers at the 2013 Boston Marathon.

Social Media and Tech

Using technology to connect people in the hours after the bombs exploded, people turned to the Internet for answers. Runners and spectators used Facebook and Twitter to tell friends and family that they were safe. Police even used social media to communicate with citizens. The Boston Globe temporarily turned its website into a live news blog. The blog linked to Twitter feeds from news outlets and authorities. The Boston Globe also posted a spreadsheet so Boston residents could sign up to help **displaced** *victims. Many needed housing, food, or transportation. In less than 30 minutes, 1,000 Bostonians had responded.*

Winners of the 2013 Boston Marathon

Hours before the bombs exploded, two winners crossed the finish line of the 2013 Boston Marathon. The male winner was Lelisa Desisa from Ethiopia. The female winner was Rita Jeptoo from Kenya. It is common for marathon winners to come from Kenya or Ethiopia. Since 1988, Ethiopian men have won the Boston Marathon 6 times. Ethiopian women have won it 7 times. Kenyan men have won the Boston Marathon 21 times. Kenyan women have won 13 times. Studies have been done on the success of runners from these countries. Scientists claim that the East African diet and high altitude are factors. Walking and running barefoot from an early age is also a factor. Runners from England, Canada, Scotland, New Zealand, and the United States train in Kenya each year. They eat the same diet as African runners and run for hours a day.

The Longest Mile

Three people were killed at the site of the bombing. Krystle Campbell went to the marathon to cheer for runners at the finish line every year. Lingzi Lu had just moved from China to Boston for **graduate school**. She and some school friends decided to watch the runners cross the finish line. Eight-year-old Martin Richard was on the sidelines with his family. More than 200 others were severely injured by the bombs. Their stories of survival are inspiring.

The Richard family was just a few feet away from one of the bombs. The explosion killed eight-year-old Martin. His younger sister Jane lost her left leg. Jane's determination and enthusiasm inspired the whole city of Boston. She received a **prosthetic** leg that allows her to walk, run, and dance. Jane sang the national

The Richard family and Boston mayor Marty Walsh walk near the finish line of the marathon on the two-year anniversary of the bombing.

anthem at a Boston Red Sox game just six months after the bombing. Jane and her family returned to the finish line on the first anniversary of the 2013 Boston Marathon for a memorial event.

Just before the first explosion, James Costello and some friends were walking toward the finish line. Costello and his friends were badly injured. His injuries required many surgeries. While in the hospital, he met Krista D'Agostino. She was one of the nurses who cared for him. The two formed a friendship while Costello was being treated at the hospital. They were later married.

Carlos Arredondo and Jeff Bauman are honored before Game Six of the 2013 Stanley Cup final.

Dancer Adrianne Haslet-Davis was a spectator at the 2013 Boston Marathon. She lost part of her left leg when the bombs exploded. She decided she would not let her injury stop her from living her life. Haslet-Davis received a prosthetic leg that was designed for dancing. A year after her injury, she returned to the stage to dance. Haslet-Davis also trained for the 2016 Boston Marathon. She ran on a special prosthetic leg made for runners.

Erin Hurley was nearing the finish line when the first of the two bombs exploded. Her boyfriend, Jeff Bauman, was there waiting for her. Bauman lost both of his lower legs in the explosion. He was taken to safety by Carlos Arredondo. Bauman received prosthetic legs and learned to walk again. He and Hurley eventually got married. But Bauman was also a hero. He had seen one of the Tsarnaev brothers place a backpack on the ground. Bauman was able to help investigators identify the two bombers.

Jeff Bauman wrote a book about his experience. It was later turned into a movie. Bauman wanted people to understand that many people were affected by the bombing. Bauman's story, and countless others, are proof that the human spirit can overcome even the biggest **obstacles**.

Running Blades

Someone who loses all or part of an arm or leg is called an amputee. Amputees are given an **artificial** limb called a prosthetic. An amputee who wants to run can get special prosthetics made for running. Running prosthetics are J- or C-shaped blades. They are made of **carbon fiber**. Running prosthetics bend slightly when the runner hits the ground. Then they return to their original shape. This motion helps amputees use less energy while running.

CHAPTER 5

Boston Strong

The Boston Marathon has been a part of the Boston community for more than 100 years. Runners bond over **shin splints** and big hills on the 26.2-mile (42.2-km) course. One million spectators line the route to encourage runners. The race brings people of all ages together every April. But the 2013 Boston Marathon brought people together in many unexpected ways. Lives were saved by total strangers. Scared runners and fans with nowhere to go found comfort from people they had never met. Ordinary people became heroes. In the days after the bombing, the city adopted the slogan "Boston Strong."

The day after the bombing, the Boston Red Sox played baseball in Cleveland, Ohio. Members of the Cleveland Indians baseball team had a jersey made. They hung the jersey in the Boston

After the bombing, "Boston Strong" became an official slogan for the city of Boston.

dugout before the game. It had the number "617" and the words "Boston Strong" on it. The number 617 is the main Boston **area code**. Someone had written a note to the Boston Red Sox team that said, "From our city to yours. Our hearts and our prayers go out to you, Boston. Love, Cleveland."

One day after the bombing, One Fund Boston was started. One Fund Boston was created to raise money for bombing victims. Within 75 days, the fund had given almost $61 million to survivors and victims' families.

On the fourth anniversary of the bombing, the Richard family gathered near the Boston **seaport**. Bombing survivor Jane Richard and her father broke ground for a new children's area. Martin's Park will honor Jane's brother Martin. The park will be wheelchair accessible. The Richard family called the park their gift to the city of Boston for the kindness shown to them after the bombing.

Meb Keflezighi

Even though they were "Boston Strong," runners and spectators at the 2014 Boston Marathon needed a reminder of hope. That hope came across the finish line wearing red, white, and blue. Meb Keflezighi was the first American to win the Boston Marathon since 1985. Keflezighi was not expected to win the marathon. He not only won, but he also achieved a personal record. Keflezighi had been a spectator at the 2013 Boston Marathon. He had vowed to compete in 2014 and run the race of his life. Keflezighi's win inspired the entire nation.

Six months after the bombing, the Boston Red Sox won the **World Series**. It was the first time the Red Sox had won a championship at home since 1918. The city held a parade to celebrate the victory. The parade paused at the finish line of the marathon. Team members remembered the victims and survivors of the bombing. Red Sox player Jonny Gomes placed the World Series trophy on the finish line. The team draped the "617 Boston Strong" jersey over the trophy. The Boston Red Sox and thousands of spectators sang "God Bless America." It was proof that the city of Boston would never stop running.

Winners of the Boston Marathon by Country

(countries with 5 or more winners)

Men's Open		Women's Open	
United States	44	United States	15
Kenya	21	Kenya	12
Canada	16	Ethiopia	7
Japan	8	Germany	5
Ethiopia	6		
Finland	7		

TIMELINE

April 15, 10:00 a.m.

The elite men and the public begin the race.

April 15, 12:10 p.m.

Men's winner Lelisa Desisa crosses the finish line.

April 15, 9:00-9:22 a.m.

The mobility impaired and wheelchair groups begin the Boston Marathon.

2013

April 15, 2:49 p.m.

Two homemade bombs explode 12 seconds apart near the finish line of the Boston Marathon.

April 15, 9:32 a.m.

The elite women begin the race.

April 15, 11:58 a.m.

Women's winner Rita Jeptoo crosses the finish line.

[21ST CENTURY SKILLS LIBRARY]

March 11

Dzhokhar is sentenced to death.

April 16

Jeff Bauman, who was injured in the explosion, gives the FBI a description of the young man who set a backpack on the ground near him.

April 19, 7:00 a.m.

Police begin going door to door in Watertown, Massachusetts, looking for Dzhokhar.

2015

April 19, 8:45 p.m.

Police arrest Dzhokhar.

April 19

The Tsarnaev brothers run from police. Tamerlan is killed by police officers, while Dzhokhar escapes in the stolen car.

April 19, 7:00 p.m.

A resident of Watertown finds a man hiding under a tarp in his boat, which is dry-docked in his backyard.

Think About It

What do you think is happening in this photo?

Look at the photo on page 11. How is that scene similar to the one in this photo? How is it different?

Do you know any police officers or fire fighters? How do they keep us safe? Why are they so important when it comes to big events like races and other sporting events?

Learn More

BOOKS

Canasi, Brittany. *Boston*. Vero Beach, FL.: Rourke Educational Media, 2016.

Challen, Paul. *Surviving the Boston Marathon Bombing*. New York: Rosen Publishing, 2016.

Wiseman, Blaine. *Boston Marathon*. New York: Weigl Publishing, 2011.

ON THE WEB

Boston Marathon Tragedy
www.factmonster.com/world/disaster-digest/boston-marathon-tragedy

Landmarks of Boston
www.factmonster.com/us/landmarks-boston

Meb Keflezighi
www.marathonmeb.com/Meb-Keflezighi

GLOSSARY

amateur (AM-uh-chur) a person who plays a sport without being paid

ancient (AYN-chent) something from the very distant past that no longer exists

annual (AN-yoo-uhl) taking place every year

area code (AIR-ee-uh KOHD) the three-digit number dialed before a telephone number

artificial (ahr-tih-FIH-shul) made by humans instead of occurring naturally

carbon fiber (KAHR-bin FAHY-bur) a very lightweight but strong man-made material

displaced (dis-PLEHYST) out of one's usual location; having no place to go

fragile (FRA-jul) damaged or hurt easily

graduate school (GRA-joo-it SKOOL) a program at a college or university offering an advanced degree

modern (MAH-durn) something happening in the present time

obstacles (AHB-stih-kuls) things that stand in someone's way

olive wreaths (AH-liv REETHS) olive branches formed into circles; prizes for the winners at the ancient Olympic Games

prosthetic (prahs-THEH-tik) a limb or other body part made with man-made materials

qualify (KWAH-lih-fai) to have the necessary score or requirements

sanction (SAYNK-shun) to officially approve

seaport (SEE-port) a location in a town or city where ships dock

shin splints (SHIN SPLINTS) pain along the inner edge of the shin bone caused by running

spectators (SPEK-tay-turz) people who watch a game or other event

sprint (SPRINT) to run very fast

tragedy (TRA-jih-dee) an accident, crime, or disaster that causes great suffering

trials (TRAI-uls) in the Olympics, a tryout event to determine placement on a team

World Series (WURLD SEER-eez) the championship tournament of Major League Baseball

INDEX